THE HOW AND WHY WONDER BOOK OF
WINNING OF THE WEST

Written by FELIX SUTTON
Illustrated by LEONARD VOSBURGH
Editorial Production: DONALD D. WOLF

Edited under the supervision of
Dr. Paul E. Blackwood,
Washington, D. C.

Text and illustrations approved by
Oakes A. White
Brooklyn Children's Museum, Brooklyn, New York

GROSSET & DUNLAP • **Publishers** • **NEW YORK**

Introduction

The greatest mass migration in world history was probably the trek of thousands of pioneers in wagon trains across mountains, plains and deserts to the wonderful new land of Oregon. But that movement was just one of the exciting probes of pioneers seeking lands, homes and riches in the West. This *How and Why Wonder Book of Winning of the West* describes the major events in our nation's growth from settling the original colonies to populating the land from the Atlantic to the Pacific.

The story could be told in terms of great names. Daniel Boone, Lewis and Clark, Kit Carson, Brigham Young, Thomas Jefferson, Davy Crockett, Buffalo Bill Cody, and Leland Stanford are just a few people who suggest the bravery, wisdom and foresightedness of the early leaders.

The story could also be told in terms of the kinds of transportation available. Such a story would feature the horse, wagon train, pony express, bull train, stage coach and steam engine. Or finally, the story could be told in terms of the kinds of people that characterized this period in our history — mountain men, river pirates, forty-niners, Indians, "bad men," cowboys, homesteaders, and religious sects.

All of these kinds of people, specific men, and the movements of which they were a part are blended into an exciting story in this *How and Why Wonder Book of Winning of the West*. The book is an essential addition to the history library of school boys and girls.

Paul E. Blackwood

Dr. Blackwood is a professional employee in the U. S. Office of Education. This book was edited by him in his private capacity and no official support or endorsement by the Office of Education is intended or should be inferred.

Library of Congress Catalogue Card Number: 63-9531

Contents

In the beginning of the 17th century, the tiny Mayflower brought to America 102 English Pilgrims who had left their country to find religious freedom. They were the first English settlers of what is today Massachusetts and other parts of New England.

A house and fort exactly like those built by the Pilgrims stand in Plymouth today. ➪

This is a scene of the interior of an early settler's house in Vermont. ➪

Plymouth Rock, now covered by a portico, is traditionally considered the place where the Pilgrims first set foot on land. The date of their landing was carved into the stone much later.

Hunters brought home turkey for the first Thanksgiving which was observed in Plymouth in 1621.

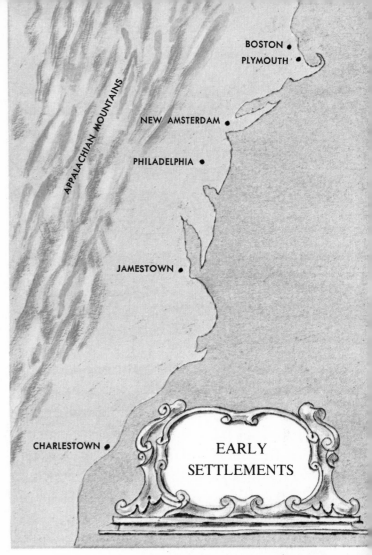

The map shows the location of the early settlements. New York, of course, was still New Amsterdam.

The Early Settlements in America

When the first colonists came from Europe to what is now the United States, they settled in small communities along the Atlantic coast. Usually these settlements were located at or near the mouths of big rivers — the Charles and the Connecticut in New England, the Hudson in New York, the James, the Potomac, and the Roanoke in Virginia.

What was the first frontier?

Behind these first settlements, reaching out toward the west, a vast primitive forest loomed up like a great green wall that extended into the setting sun. These deep, dark woods were wild and free, and they abounded in all kinds of game. Large herds of deer and bison roamed through the woodland paths. Grouse and partridge were as thick as songbirds. Clouds of passenger pigeons darkened the sky.

All that a man had to do to make a home for his family was to mark out a few acres of woodland on the edge of the forest and clear away the trees. Then he planted corn and beans, Indian style, between the stumps. From the logs he built a crude cabin, and fashioned tables and chairs.

For the most part the land was free to any man who wanted to clear it. If a man was a good hunter and a hard worker, he usually had little difficulty in keeping the family larder filled. But the heavy, almost trackless forest, teeming with wild Indians and wild beasts, acted as a natural barrier to the West. Only a few of the more adventurous hunters penetrated very far into it.

Then more and more of the oppressed people of Europe, lured by the promise of free land and freedom of religion, sought refuge in the New World. Gradually the seacoast settlements became crowded, and the settlers began to move farther west. This was the first trickle of the vast flow of westward migration that was to continue for more than two hundred years and finally populate our country from coast to coast.

After the coastal forests had been penetrated, and farmlands had been cleared many miles inland from the sea, still another great barrier remained. This was the Appalachian Mountains, a long, twisting range extending from Canada almost down to the Gulf of Mexico.

What was the mountain barrier?

In those days there were, of course, no roads. It was impossible to get over the mountains except on foot. Still only the most hard-bitten hunters and the adventurers who wanted "to see what lay over the next ridge" wandered across them.

There was a lot of country between the Atlantic Ocean and the Appalachians, and the people spread all through it. What at first had been outpost clearings in the woods, rapidly became open farm lands. Towns sprang up and the settlements became colonies of England. Almost before the people realized it, a new and growing nation had been created. And its frontier lay always toward the west.

The tasks of a pioneer woman were not confined to the house. Tilling the soil was a difficult, but not unusual, job for her.

How Did the Early Pioneers Live?

The first settlers in the American wilderness needed only two basic tools to survive. One was a gun and the other was an ax. With his gun, a man hunted game and protected his family from hostile Indians. With his ax, he chopped down trees to clear land for planting, and trimmed logs to build his cabin.

The guns that the original settlers brought from Europe **What was a "long rifle?"** were crude blunderbusses, smooth-bore muskets like those used by European armies. To hit a single target with such a gun was almost impossible, and it soon became obvious that it was of little use to a hunter in the thick North American woods.

A group of German gunsmiths had settled in Pennsylvania, and it was not long before they had designed a gun that was ideal for the woodsman's needs. It was relatively light, and its long, rifled barrel made it highly accurate. It was, in fact, one of the most accurate guns ever made, including many modern rifles of today. With it, a good marksman could shoot a squirrel in the eye at a hundred yards.

This gun quickly became famous as the Pennsylvania rifle. Then Daniel Boone carried it into the new land of Kentucky, and it was called the Kentucky rifle. But by whatever name this rifle was known, it was a prime factor in the early winning of the West — just as the Colt revolver and the Winchester carbine were to be a century later.

We think of the log cabin as being typically American, a **Who invented the log cabin?** symbol of the western frontier. But when the first settlers came to the New World,

The Pennsylvania rifle, one of the most accurate guns ever made, was a settler's best weapon to defend his home and family against all kinds of attacks.

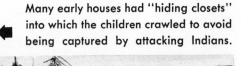

Many early houses had "hiding closets" into which the children crawled to avoid being captured by attacking Indians.

they built houses of woven branches covered by reeds and dried grass. It never occurred to them to make use of the timber that grew in such profusion all around them.

The Swedish colonists brought the log cabin to America. This was the type of house in which they had lived in Scandanavia, and the American forests provided limitless building materials. With no tools except a good ax, a Swede could put up a snug, weatherproof cabin in only a few days.

Because it was so practical, the idea of the log cabin quickly became popular with all the other settlers. Very soon hardly any other kind of home was to be seen on America's rapidly developing western frontier.

Swedish colonists brought the log cabin to America.

One of the great social occasions of the frontier was the "house-raising." This was one of the many ways that the early settlers had of helping each other make life easier in the primitive forest.

What was a house-raising?

After a man had selected a site for his new home, he cut and trimmed all the logs he would need for his house, his barn, and his corncrib. Then, when everything was ready, all of his neighbors for miles around came to spend the day, bringing their wives and children with them.

Some of the men notched the logs so that they would fit smoothly together. Others raised them into position to make the walls. Still others sawed

planks to make window frames and doors. The most skillful axmen cut shingles for the roof. The chimney was made of stones, or of sticks held together with clay.

The men joked and shouted as they worked, and the cabin went up quickly. Long before nightfall, everyone was usually ready for the feast that the women had prepared and laid out on long luncheon tables before the new cabin's door. There were piles of venison steaks, bear steaks, roast turkeys, and steaming dishes of beans, potatoes and corn.

Then, after the remains of the meal had been cleared away, the fiddlers tuned up their instruments and everyone danced the picturesque square dances

After a full days work and a hearty meal, the fiddlers appeared, and everybody danced until the early hours of the new day.

of the frontier until the moon had gone down and the morning star rose high in the sky.

Life on the frontier was hard and dangerous, but the people always managed to take a little time out for fun.

9

Daniel Boone

One of the first, and today the most famous, of the early pioneers who led the way westward over the barrier of the Appalachian Mountains, was a man named Daniel Boone. He was a farmer in the Yadkin Valley of North Carolina. But he was also the kind of person that folks called "fiddle-footed." In the language of that day and time, this meant that he was never content to stay very long in one place. Every year he made long hunting trips deep into the western mountains.

What was the "Dark and Bloody Ground?"

Ever since he had been a boy, Daniel had heard stories of a fabulous country that lay on the other side of the mountains. Hunters and trappers called it Kaintuck. The Indians called it "The Dark and Bloody Ground." Today we know it as the state of Kentucky.

Kentucky was alive with game. Its trees were unbelievably huge. The soil of its broad meadows was lavishly rich. Both the Shawnees and the Cherokees claimed it, but neither tribe lived on it. Instead they used it as their hunting ground, as did the Choctaws, the Chickasaws, and the Creeks. And whenever two parties of the rival tribes met, it also became a battle ground. In this way Kentucky earned its Indian name.

The only trouble was that the mountains guarded it like a protecting wall. There was no way for white people to get over them with wagons and supplies.

One day, in the spring of 1767, an old hunter friend, John Finley, stopped by the Boone cabin in North Carolina.

"I've just come back from another trip to Kaintuck, Dan'l," he said. "It's as pretty as it ever was, and the deer and buffalo are even thicker. The country is just begging for white men to come in and settle it."

"Did you find a gap through the mountains?" Daniel asked.

"No," Finley replied. "I went up to Virginia and floated a canoe down the Ohio. But I heard Indian tales of a gap that would be big enough to take wagons through. The tribes call it the Warrior's Path."

"Then let's go and find it," said Daniel Boone.

A few days later, Daniel, Finley and four other men loaded pack horses with supplies and set out to find a way into Kentucky. For weeks they traveled northwest, picking their way through the heavy forests and over the towering mountains. Finally they came to a well-worn trail that wound its way between two ridges that loomed up on either side.

Daniel and his companions were jubilant. At last they had found the Warrior's Path. They renamed it the Cumberland Gap. It was the gateway to the promised land of Kentucky!

The six men hunted all summer, and by **What did Daniel Boone find in Kentucky?** the time the first winds of approaching winter began to chill the mountain air, their camp was piled high with the skins of bear, deer, foxes, beaver and buffalo. These would bring extremely high prices back in the eastern colonies. The hunters had several encounters with wandering Indian parties, but always managed to escape because they had become better woodsmen than the redskins.

Then one day in late fall, when it was time to take their catch back through the Gap, they returned to camp in the evening to find that it had been raided by the Indians. Every one of their valuable skins had been stolen, as well as most of their pack horses. Their long summer's work had gone for nothing.

It was a severe blow, but nothing could be done about it. They had to leave before the winter snows closed up the Cumberland Gap. But Daniel Boone shook his head. "You boys go on back home," he said. "Injuns or no Injuns, I like this country and I want to see more of it. Just leave me a supply of powder and ball. I'm going to winter here."

And that is what he did. All that winter, and the next spring and summer and fall too, he hunted alone through the forests and plains of Kentucky. He explored its rivers, its valleys and its mountains. And the more he saw of this beautiful land, the more he was convinced that he wanted to make it his home.

Finally, after almost two years of exploring, he returned to his little farm in the Yadkin Valley. Now he was obsessed with a great idea. He was determined to lead a group of settlers through

Shawnee Indians raided the camp of Daniel Boone's party and took all the valuable skins they could find.

During the meeting of the Indian chiefs with Judge Henderson and Daniel Boone, "The Dark and Bloody Ground," today the state of Kentucky, was bought.

the Cumberland Gap and into the new western country.

There was one man who was particularly interested in Daniel's plan. He was Richard Henderson, a colonel of the North Carolina militia and the local judge. His idea was to buy the hunting ground from the Indians and open it up to settlers.

What was the Wilderness Road?

Daniel arranged a meeting between the Indian chiefs and Judge Henderson. And there, under the branches of a spreading sycamore tree on the banks of the Watauga River, the white men bought "The Dark and Bloody Ground," in return for a great store of blankets, guns, powder, lead, knives, cloth, beads and other trinkets.

After the meeting was over, Daniel gathered together a group of men and began the long and difficult job of cutting a wagon road through the woods, through the Cumberland Gap, and up the Kentucky River. After the two years he had spent exploring Kentucky, Daniel knew all the deer paths and "buffalo streets" that wound their way over the mountains. Slowly chopping their way through the dense forest, the men cleared the great route known as the Wilderness Road. This was the highway that first opened the way for settlers to drive their wagons over the mountain barrier toward the West. (See map on opposite page.)

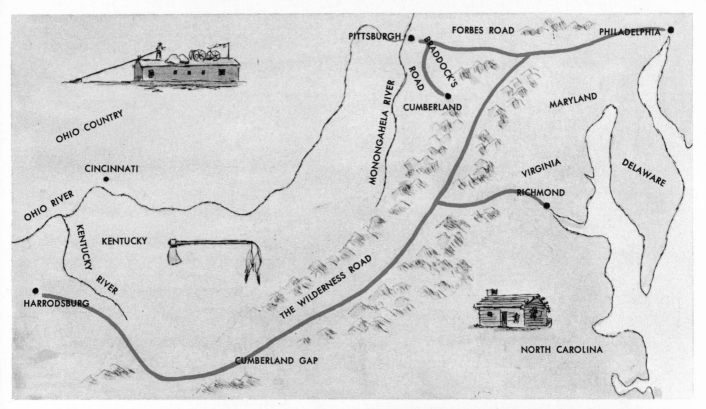

The Pennsylvania Roads were a big factor in the westward movement.

The Pennsylvania Roads and River Highways

Where was Fort Duquesne? At about the same time that Daniel Boone was leading the way across the southern mountains to Kentucky, a handful of hardy pioneers was also drifting westward through the hills of Pennsylvania.

In 1755, during the French and Indian War, General Edward Braddock led a force of British regulars and colonial militia in an attempt to capture the French stronghold of Fort Duquesne. This fort was located at the forks of the Ohio River, on the site of the present city of Pittsburgh. In order to move the army and its supplies, Braddock's men laboriously hacked out a crude roadway through the thick woods. They had progressed as far as the Monongahela Valley when they were ambushed by a large force of French soldiers and Indian warriors and all but wiped out. Braddock himself was killed. About the only people who managed to escape with their lives were American woodsmen under the com-

In an attempt to take Fort Duquesne in 1755, General Edward Braddock's men cleared a crude roadway that later was known as the Wilderness Road.

13

mand of a young Virginia officer named George Washington.

A few years later, Colonel John Forbes cut another road westward from Harrisburg in a second attempt to take Fort Duquesne. The French burned and abandoned Duquesne before Forbes' army reached it, and Forbes built Fort Pitt at the river forks. Fort Pitt was later renamed Pittsburgh.

It was over the remains of these two primitive roads that the first few Pennsylvania pioneers made their way west.

The American Revolution, which began in 1775, pretty much put a stop to the western flow of migration. The colonists were too busy fighting for their freedom from the English king to think about expansion. But after the war had been won, and the United States was at last an independent nation, the movement of the people westward suddenly swelled from a trickle to a flood. The young country was flexing its new-found muscles. And as always, the stream of population flowed towards the west.

Braddock's road had long since been abandoned and swallowed up once more by the forest. But in 1783, the underbrush clogging up Forbes road over the years was cleared, and soon wagon trains were banging and bumping across its uneven surface towards the Ohio River. The modern Pennsylvania Turnpike, a fast four-lane superhighway over which you can speed from Harrisburg to Pittsburgh in only a few hours, follows the general route of Colonel Forbes' original mountain road. In 1783, however, the journey took not hours, but weeks and even months.

What were the river highways? During the American Revolution, most of the colonies along the Eastern seaboard had promised grants of land in the western territories to their soldiers as a reward for military service. In addition, the new government sold vast tracts of land in western Virginia, Ohio, Illinois and Indiana for as little as a few cents an acre. Ownership required only that the settler build a cabin on his land and clear at least a part of it for farming.

Since Forbes Road and Boone's Wilderness Trace were the only wagon trails that had been even partially cleared through the dense forest, the broad Ohio River was the natural highway upon which the immigrants to these new lands could travel. Pittsburgh became the jumping-off place into the vast wilderness country.

RAFT

All kinds of boats on the Mississippi river carried the products of the Mississippi and Ohio valleys to the markets.

A man would take his family and all his worldly possessions, including cows, pigs, poultry, oxen and horses, over Forbes Road to Pittsburgh. There, several pioneer families would join together and build a flatboat to float down the river. If they were extremely poor, as most of the pioneers were, they would fell trees and saw them into planks by hand. If they had a little money, as few did, they could buy the planks from sawmills in Pittsburgh. Or, if they were relatively wealthy, as very, very few were, they could buy the boats already built.

What was an ark?

These riverboats were huge, clumsy craft called arks. An ark was anywhere from twenty to sixty feet long and proportionately wide. Its entire deckspace was usually covered by a large cabin. The inside of this cabin was divided into two sections, one for the people and the other for the animals. Chicken coops and pig sties were built on the cabin's roof. Here plows and other farm tools that the settlers took with them were stored, plus the wheels and iron parts for the wagons which they would build when they reached their destination.

Some of these emigrants stopped off near the Ohio River settlements of Marietta or Kanawha. Others went farther south to Kentucky. A few bravely took their crude boats up such tributary rivers as the Miami and the Wabash to settle in the great unexplored inland forest.

Where did the pioneers settle?

Floating a big awkward ark down a river was difficult enough, and it ordinarily took three or four strong men to

KEEL BOAT

FLAT BOAT

ARK

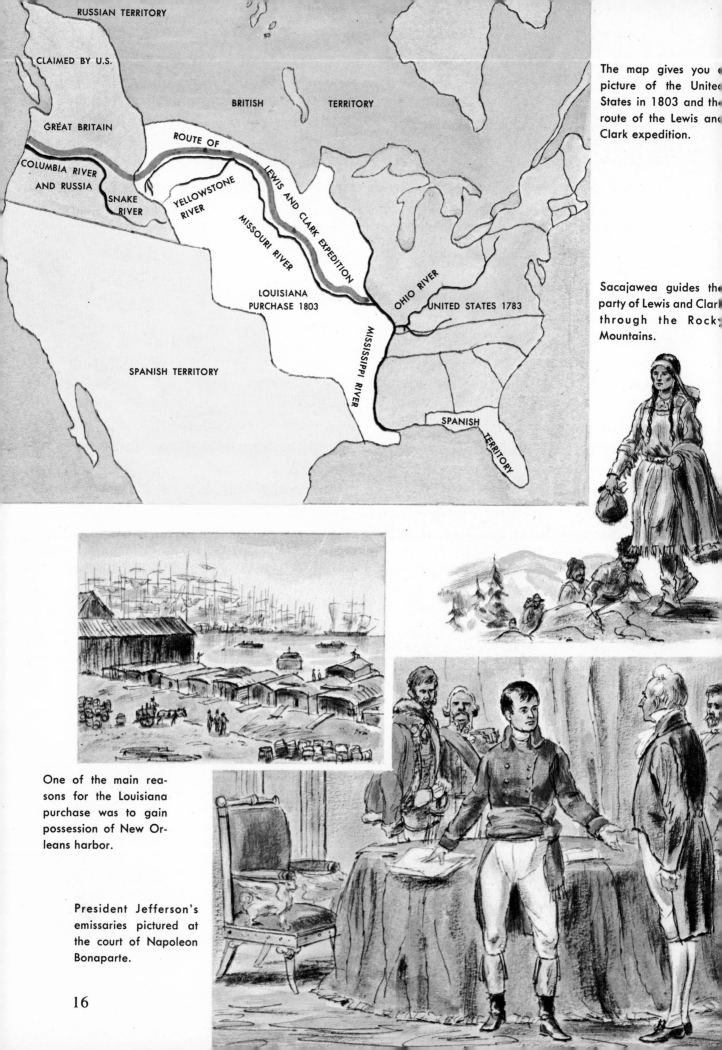

RUSSIAN TERRITORY

CLAIMED BY U.S.

BRITISH TERRITORY

GREAT BRITAIN

ROUTE OF

COLUMBIA RIVER AND RUSSIA

SNAKE RIVER

YELLOWSTONE RIVER

LEWIS AND CLARK EXPEDITION

MISSOURI RIVER

OHIO RIVER

LOUISIANA PURCHASE 1803

UNITED STATES 1783

MISSISSIPPI RIVER

SPANISH TERRITORY

SPANISH TERRITORY

The map gives you a picture of the United States in 1803 and the route of the Lewis and Clark expedition.

Sacajawea guides the party of Lewis and Clark through the Rocky Mountains.

One of the main reasons for the Louisiana purchase was to gain possession of New Orleans harbor.

President Jefferson's emissaries pictured at the court of Napoleon Bonaparte.

do it. But taking it *up* a river was a task that today seems almost impossible. The crews managed to accomplish this by staying close to the bank where the current was slowest, and then rowing, poling, and pulling the boat along by a strong tow rope. Sometimes they were lucky if they made a mile in a day.

Aside from the natural hazards of river travel — floods, swift currents, rapids and hidden snags — the early settlers of the Midwest faced two more dangers that were even worse. One was the hostile Indian, and the other was the river pirate.

Who were the river pirates?

The Indians naturally resented the intrusion of the white men into their hunting grounds, and they attacked them whenever they had the chance. River travelers soon learned that it was almost suicide to tie up for the night to a tree on the river bank. Instead, they anchored their arks in the middle of the stream. Even so, bands of Indians would come out in canoes and attack under cover of darkness. A sharp vigil had to be kept at all times. Fortunately for the settlers, few of the Indians had guns at that time, and their bows and arrows were no match for river boatmen well armed with Kentucky rifles.

Much more dangerous than Indians were the river pirates. These were gangs of ruthless criminals who usually made their headquarters at bends in the river where the going was always difficult. When they spotted a riverboat, they quickly rowed out to it in small boats, killed the passengers, threw their bodies overboard, and then took the ark downriver to sell its cargo in the southern settlements. Since the pirates almost always out-numbered the crews of the riverboats, it was a rare and lucky group of pioneers who managed to escape once they were attacked.

But in spite of all the dangers, the people of the new United States kept on moving from the crowded eastern seacoast toward the wide-open West. It was a mass movement that nothing could stop.

The Louisiana Purchase

In the year 1803, the United States looked much as it is pictured on the map that appears on the opposite page. Except for Florida, which was still a Spanish colony, almost all of the land from the Atlantic coast westward to the Mississippi River

What new western lands did it open up?

was a part of the newly created United States. The entire middle section of the country — from the Gulf of Mexico north to the Canadian border, and from the Mississippi west to the Rocky Mountains — belonged to France. This vast territory was known as Louisiana.

Southwest of Louisiana, the area now occupied by the states of California, Ne-

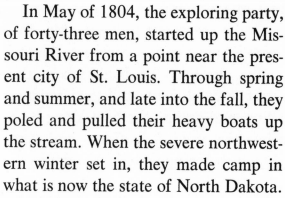

vada, Utah, Arizona, Colorado, New Mexico and Texas, was a Spanish possession called New Spain. The present states of Oregon and Washington were part of British Canada.

Then, in 1803, President Thomas Jefferson sent a mission to Paris to try to buy the town of New Orleans from the French. Since most of the produce of the western settlements was floated down the Mississippi and sold in New Orleans, the President felt that the town would be more prosperous in American hands.

But Napoleon Bonaparte, who had become emperor of France, surprised the American ambassador. Napoleon was then embroiled in a war with England, and needed money much more than he needed a piece of the North American wilderness. So he offered to sell not only New Orleans, but the entire Louisiana Territory. His asking price was roughly fifteen million dollars. Jefferson, with Senate approval, quickly accepted this offer, and by one stroke of the pen, the total area of the United States was more than doubled. This transaction has become known as the Louisiana Purchase.

Who were Lewis and Clark?

SCOUT

The ink was no sooner dry on the Louisiana Purchase pact, than President Jefferson dispatched a party to explore the new regions which had been added to the United States. For its leader, he selected Captain Meriwether Lewis, an army officer who was also the President's private secretary. For his co-captain, Lewis chose Captain William Clark.

In May of 1804, the exploring party, of forty-three men, started up the Missouri River from a point near the present city of St. Louis. Through spring and summer, and late into the fall, they poled and pulled their heavy boats up the stream. When the severe northwestern winter set in, they made camp in what is now the state of North Dakota.

The following April as soon as the snows melted, the Lewis and Clark party moved on toward the West. By this time they had acquired the services of a young Indian girl, named Sacajawea, as a guide. Carrying a papoose in a cradle on her back, Sacajawea led the explorers across the Montana plains, over the Rocky Mountains, to the great Columbia River which tumbles down the western side of the Continental Divide to empty into the Pacific Ocean.

In November of 1805, Lewis and Clark built Fort Clatsop on the Pacific Coast. They thus became the first Americans to travel all the way across America from ocean to ocean. During the winter, the two captains made detailed maps of their route across the continent. In spring they started the long journey back, arriving in St. Louis in September, 1806, after travelling for two and a half years.

The Lewis and Clark Expedition, probing as it did into lands that were completely unknown, revealed all of the far West to the American people. It would be many years before the westward flow of population would follow. But Meriwether Lewis and William Clark had shown them the way. (See map on page 16 for the route of the expedition.)

Having traced the Missouri to its source, Lewis and Clark went beyond the Louisiana purchase territory and finally reached the Columbia River in 1805.

The Mountain Men

After Lewis and Clark had opened the pathway to the great wide-open spaces of the West, a new breed of pioneers began to infiltrate the western mountains and plains. These pioneers were not permanent settlers intent upon creating homes and farms. Instead, they were nomadic hunters and trappers known as "mountain men."

What were they hunting?

The western wilderness was teeming with fur-bearing animals — mink, fox, otter, bear, buffalo, and beaver. Of these, the last two were by far the most important commercially. During the early years of the 1800s, every stylish gentleman both in the eastern states and in Europe wore a hat made of beaver fur. Lap robes made of buffalo hide were standard equipment on all fashionable buggies and sleighs. Therefore, the trade in these two furs was booming, and the mountain men were willing to endure great hardships to obtain them.

A mountain man usually worked alone or in the company of his Indian wife. All year long he labored at the dangerous and lonesome job of killing buffalo and trapping beaver and other animals. Then, usually in the summer, he journeyed to a prearranged place, sometimes hundreds of miles away from his trapping grounds, to meet with the fur traders to sell his year's catch and to have a reunion with other mountain men. This sort of meeting was called a "rendezvous."

The rendezvous was the one bright spot in the mountain man's solitary year. First, he sold his year's accumulation of furs and bought the few supplies like lead, gunpowder, tobacco, and new

19

traps that he would need for the next twelve months. Then he normally plunged into a gigantic binge of drinking and gambling that ended only when most of his money was gone.

After the fun was over, and the mountain man was once again "broke," he strapped his meager supplies on his pack horse and went back into the wilderness to work hard for another year. The traders returned to civilization with not only all the mountain men's furs, but also with most of the money that they had paid for them. No wonder their profitable business flourished.

The mountain men took millions upon millions of dollars worth of valuable furs out of the west. But there is no record that any of them kept more than a few pennies from their profits.

The mountain men made no permanent settlements. But they did make one important contribution to the winning of the West. In their wanderings, they discovered trails through the western valleys, and passes over the Rocky Mountains that were later used by the pioneers who trekked westward to settle the Pacific coast.

This is a picture of a typical mountain man in about the year 1830. He wore a fringed **How did a mountain man dress?** hunting shirt and fringed trousers of deerskin. His moccasins were the same as those of the western Indians. He allowed his hair and beard to grow long. Both were ordinarily trimmed only at

The "rendezvous" of the mountain men shows fur trading and fun in full swing.

At right, beaver trap, skinning knife and a beaver skin.

BEAVER TRAP

KNIFE

BEAVER SKIN

horn and his "war-bag" were slung over his shoulder. The war-bag contained lead for bullets, a bullet mold, flint and steel for making fire, and now and then the scalp of an Indian that he had been forced to kill to save his own life. He carried a tomahawk and a broad-bladed hunting knife tucked into his belt.

Perhaps next to the cowboy of fifty years later, the mountain man was the most picturesque of all the Americans who played a part in the final winning of the West.

Two of the most famous of the mountain men were Kit Carson and Jim Bridger. Both had western towns named after them — Carson City, Nevada, and Bridger, Wyoming.

rendezvous time, and sometimes not at all. He usually wore a conspicuous hat made of beaver or raccoon skin.

The mountain man carried a Kentucky rifle under his arm. A powder

The Oregon Trail

What was the Willamette?

The first travelers to follow the footsteps of Lewis and Clark to the Oregon Country were Christian missionaries. Their purpose was to convert the Indians to the white man's religion. One of these men, a young Methodist minister named Jason Lee, established a mission in the valley of the Willamette River, which flows northward to the Columbia.

The Willamette was then, as it is today, one of the loveliest and most fertile valleys in America. It was blessed with plenty of rainfall, and a mild climate. Great fir tree woods covered its hilly slopes, and its broad mountain meadows were billowing seas of grass.

A year or two after Jason Lee had founded his mission, he went back east to give lectures in order to raise funds for more missions. His eloquent descriptions of the valley fired up audiences at every place he spoke. Oregon seemed like the Promised Land, just as Kentucky had seemed half a century before.

By the mid-1840s a torrent of emigrants was flowing west. But this time they were not just going from North Carolina or Virginia to Kentucky. They were united in a mass movement to take their wagons some 2,500 miles over untried trails, across the plains and deserts and over the Rockies, to the wonderful new land of Oregon.

The fact that the Oregon Country was a sort of no-man's-land, claimed by both Great Britain and the United States, did not bother these eager land seekers. Independence and Saint Joseph, in Missouri, were the usual jumping-off places. There the people gathered by the thousands to form into wagon trains to travel the long road to the west. This movement turned out to be probably the greatest mass migration in world history.

What was a wagon train like?

The wagon trains were organized more or less along military lines. The emigrants elected captains to command various elements of the train, and a wagon master who was in supreme command of the whole expedition. For scouts and guides, they usually employed experienced mountain men who knew by long practice

LOCATION MAP OF OREGON TRAIL

OREGON CITY
FT. BOISE
FT. HALL
FT. BRIDGER
SOUTH PASS
FT. LARAMIE
COUNCIL BLUFFS
ST. JOSEPHS
FT. KEARNEY
SALT LAKE CITY
INDEPENDENCE

Above, the wagon train in motion, and at right, the train camp attacked by hostile Indians.

The wagons were arranged in a circle for protection at night. This made the camp easier to defend during attacks.

the best trails across the plains and through the mountain passes.

The wagons were extremely sturdy vehicles, with extra-wide wheels for easier passage over mud or sand. Commonly known as "prairie schooners," the wagons were domed by canvas covers as protection against the rain, the cold, and the heat of the desert sun. Many of the owners painted signs on the canvas covers of their wagons such as: "OREGON OR BUST." Because of the hardships of the trail, a great many of the prairie schooners "busted" before they ever got to Oregon.

Every man's wagon carried all his family's possessions — furniture, farm tools, and treasured family heirlooms. It also carried barrels of flour, beans and other staple foods including water kegs. Some of the wagons were pulled by teams of horses; others were pulled by oxen. Oxen were preferred because they were more durable draft animals than horses and, in an emergency, they could be eaten as food. (So, of course, could horses, but beef tastes better than horse-meat.) The ordinary wagon train progressed at a speed of about ten or twelve miles a day.

Travelling across the Oregon Trail was a long and arduous journey. Starting at Independence or St. Joe, the trail followed the Platte River to Scott's Bluff and Fort Laramie. Then it went up and over the Continental Divide, past Fort Bridger and Fort Hall, into Idaho. From Fort Boise, it twisted through the Blue Mountains to the Columbia, to the Willamette Valley and on to the Pacific.

Where did the Oregon Trail go?

Many of the emigrants who took the Oregon Trail were buried in lonely graves beside it along the way. Some died of disease; others died from the arrows of the hostile Plains Indians. But the ones who made it had indeed found a Promised Land.

It was largely due to the presence of so many Americans in the Willamette Valley, that the boundary dispute between Great Britain and the United States was settled by treaty in favor of the United States in 1846. In 1848, Oregon became a U.S. Territory, and in 1859 it was admitted into the Union as the 33rd state.

SANTA ANNA

SAM HOUSTON

The Mexican War

During the 1820s and '30s, a large number of Americans had drifted westward from the southern states onto the broad plains of the Mexican province of Texas. There in that new, raw land they established ranches and farms.

What did the United States gain from it?

These Texans, or Texicans as they were then called, considered themselves to be Americans even though they were living on Mexican soil. As such, they resented having to submit to the tyrannical laws of the Mexican government.

24

The battle of the Alamo.

In 1836, they revolted and set up their own government.

In the first major fight of the Texas War for Independence, at the Alamo in San Antonio, some 150 Texans, including the famous scout Davy Crockett, were killed by an army of 4,000 soldiers under the command of General Santa Anna. A few months later, the ragtag-and-bobtail Texas army commanded by Sam Houston, caught Santa Anna's army off guard and thoroughly defeated it. Thereupon, Texas declared herself an independent republic. The new nation was recognized by the United States, England and France. But the government of Mexico insisted that it was still a Mexican province.

This uneasy situation existed for about nine years. Then the Texans decided that they would be better off as a part of the United States, and applied for admission to the Union. This request was granted, and Texas became our 28th state. President James Knox Polk then dispatched an American army to the Rio Grande to protect these new American citizens. Mexico considered this to be an act of war, and thus the Mexican War began.

Two years later, the war ended in an American victory. What had formerly been the territory of New Spain, was ceded to the United States. And now our country extended triumphantly from the Atlantic to the Pacific, and from the Rio Grande to Canada. The people from the crowded East swarmed like hungry locusts into these great new empty lands.

The Mormon Trek

One of the great migrations toward the vast, uncharted wilderness of the West took place in the years between the land rush to Oregon and the later gold rush to California. This was the Mormon Trek that ended in the desert of Utah. The Mormons were not seeking new land for the sake of the land itself, nor for the riches of the gold fields. Like the Pilgrims of 200 years before, they were searching for religious freedom.

Who were the Mormons?

In 1830, a man named Joseph Smith

organized a new religion. He called it the Church of Jesus Christ of Latter-day Saints. Its bible was the Book of Mormon which Smith said he had translated from golden plates given to him by an angel of the Lord. He proclaimed that he himself was a Prophet and that each member of the new church was a Saint.

The Mormon Church grew rapidly and soon had thousands of members. The leader decided to establish a colony in Ohio. But the Saints had ideas that did not conform to the way in which the other people of the Ohio country lived. They kept to themselves, and refused to associate with their neighbors or to do business with them. They established a sort of communal form of government in which every family shared and shared alike.

In addition — and this was unthinkable to the staid Christians of the frontier — they believed that a man was entitled to marry as many wives as he wished.

As a result, the Mormons were evicted from Ohio, and went west to Illinois, where they founded the town of Nauvoo.

In Illinois, as in Ohio, they met with resentment and opposition. The antagonism toward the Mormons finally grew so great that Joseph Smith was thrown into jail. While he was in his cell, a mob of masked men broke into the jailhouse one night and murdered him.

The man who succeeded Smith as the leader of the church was Brigham Young. After the Prophet's murder, Young declared that the Mormons would have to locate their colony in the unoccupied lands of the West, where there would be no other people to molest them.

The great Mormon migration began in March of 1846. Some of the Saints went in wagons pulled by oxen or horses. Others had only hand-carts, two-wheeled vehicles which were dragged across the plains and over the mountains by the men and women themselves. The Mormon band crossed the broad Missouri, struggled through the great empty prairies of Nebraska and over the mountains of Wyoming. At Fort Bridger, on the Oregon Trail, they turned southwest.

Where did the great Mormon migration go?

"There is nothing down that way but sand, saltwater, cactus and rattlesnakes," the old mountain man, Jim Bridger, warned Brigham Young. But the Mormon leader was determined to find a place as far beyond civilization as possible. He gave the command to go forward.

The country became rougher and more difficult to penetrate. Sometimes the train of wagons and hand-carts had to stop and make temporary camps while the men cleared roads through the rock-filled canyons. Then one morning, the leading wagon topped a rise, and Brigham Young looked down on the valley of the Great Salt Lake.

It was desolate land, just as Jim Bridger had said. There was no vegetation except cactus, sagebrush, and windblown tumbleweed. This was not fertile green earth, but a lifeless desert. In the distance, the iron-gray waters of the salty inland sea shimmered in the autumn sun.

But Brigham Young was satisfied. Waving his hand out over the empty valley, he spoke his historic words: *"This is the place."* It had been a year and a half since they had left Nauvoo.

In spite of the desolation of the desert,

How did the Mormons make the desert fertile?

the Mormons went to work. They dug irrigation ditches to water their crops. They built a church, and hundreds of adobe shanties to live in. They pastured their herds of cattle on the skimpy clumps of desert grass. Somehow, they managed to live through the harsh Utah winter.

By the following summer, they had dug hundreds of miles of irrigation ditches and canals that transformed the desert into fertile fields and orchards. Then, just as the crop was ready

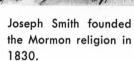

Below, Brigham Young succeeded Smith as the leader of the Mormons after Smith had been murdered.

Joseph Smith founded the Mormon religion in 1830.

Below, part of Salt Lake City in the middle of the 19th century.

A Mormon handcart train on the trek to religious freedom.

for the harvest, calamity struck. A great swarm of millions of grasshoppers rode down the wind from out of nowhere and began to consume every growing plant in sight. The people were powerless to do anything about them. It seemed as if all of their hard work had gone for nothing.

But on the heels of the calamity came a miracle. On the same wind out of nowhere came a vast flock of seagulls. The thousands of gulls greedily ate the millions of grasshoppers, and the crops were saved. The Saints were convinced that they had had at last found Zion, their Promised Land.

Today, Utah is one of the great western states of our Union, and Salt Lake City, the original Mormon settlement, is its capital. In the main square of the city is a tall monument, on top of which is the carved figure of a seagull.

The Gold Rush

In the year of 1848, California was almost as remote from the eastern United States as were the mountains of the moon. A few settlers had ventured there by ship around Cape Horn. A few others had followed the Oregon Trail as far as Fort Hall in Idaho, and then decided to turn southwest through Nevada to the new settlement of Sacramento, where the earth was reported to be so rich that crops sprang up almost overnight. But for almost all of its length and breadth of forested mountains, rushing rivers, fertile valleys and blistering deserts, California was unknown.

What happened at Sutter's mill?

Then one morning, a man named Jim Marshall was digging a ditch at Sutter's Mill, on the American River which races down out of the high Sierras. As he was working, he saw a shiny, yellow stone. He picked it up and looked at it closely. He knew at once that it must be a nugget of gold, for he had often heard the Mexicans talk of finding gold in California's streams.

Jim hurried to his boss, John Sutter, with his gleaming stone. The two gave the nugget every acid test known for gold. When they had finished, there was no doubt that Marshall had the real thing.

But instead of being elated that gold had been found on his land, Sutter was disturbed. He realized that when news of the find got out, gold-seekers by the thousands would be swarming over his fine farmland. So he pledged Marshall to keep the whole thing a secret.

At left, gold mining with a "long tom," a specially arranged set of boxes with strainers. The miners shoveled dirt that they hoped contained gold into the boxes, while a constant flow of water dissolved the dirt into mud. The mud was stirred continually and washed through the strainers, leaving gold, if there was any, on the bottom.

Panning for gold was a tiresome operation. A shallow pan was filled with silt and water from a stream and rotated gently just beneath the surface of the flowing water. The motion washed the light particles over the low rim of the pan, leaving only large pebbles and gold dust. But very often nothing except a stiff back and disappointment remained.

But keeping a gold strike a secret has always been next to impossible, and within a few months the great news had been published in newspapers as far away as New York. Just as Sutter had feared, prospectors poured in from the east to the valleys of the American, the Feather, and all the other California rivers. Most of them came by wagon train over the old Oregon Trail as far as Fort Smith, and then south to Sacramento and San Francisco. They struggled through the waterless deserts, fought their way through Indian country, and hauled their wagons over the mountain ranges.

Because most of the gold-seekers arrived in California in the year 1849, they have since been known as the "forty-niners."

What became of the forty-niners?

Many of the forty-niners died of hardship along the way across the country. The majority of those who made it staked out worthless claims and saw all their back-breaking work go for nothing. Some struck it rich and were cheated out of their claims.

But a very few were lucky. They found gold, managed to hang onto it, and organized large mining companies. Within a few years, the day of the lone-wolf prospector was finished, and the big companies had taken over.

John Sutter, the man on whose land the precious metal was first discovered, suffered the fate that he had anticipated. All of his fine acreage was dug up by the frantic and ruthless gold-seekers, and he died broke. As far as we know, Jim Marshall, who found the first nugget, never found another one.

But the gold-rush of '49 established California as one of the United States. It created the great city of San Francisco. It opened up the southern Pacific coast to migration from the east. It was one of the most important events in the winning of the West.

If you drive along the steep, narrow, winding road that today follows the Feather River down from the high Sierras to the Pacific coast, you may occasionally see an old man in a battered hat and faded bluejeans panning water out of the stream. He is probably the great-grandson of one of the original forty-niners, and he is looking for gold. And, amazingly enough, he still manages to find enough of the precious yellow flakes to eke out a meager living.

A typical miners' camp in the days of the gold rush.

The first bull train hauled freight between St. Joe, Missouri and San Francisco, California.

Transportation and Communication

As the stream of settlers poured from

What was a bull train?

the East to the West, the need for communication between the two sections of the growing United States became essential. Goods and people had to be transported and the mail had to go through.

One of the first of these transportation companies was a firm called Russell, Majors & Waddell. They hauled freight by bull train between St. Joe, Missouri and San Francisco.

A bull train was made up of twenty or thirty wagons pulled by oxen. The driver of each wagon was called a bull whacker. He walked beside his team and carried a long bull-whip which he cracked over his oxen's heads to keep them moving along.

The wagons looked like ordinary prairie schooners, except that they were bigger and stronger. Each of them was able to carry between three or four tons of freight. These trains were the first regularly scheduled transportation to the West.

The first cross-country stagecoach line

What was a stagecoach?

was established by a man named John Butterfield in 1858. The coaches were called "Concords" because most of them were built in Concord, New Hampshire. Six horses pulled the stages at an average speed of about five miles an hour. There was room inside the Concord for nine passengers. Sometimes other passengers rode on top of the coach behind the driver and the ever-present shotgun guard. Mail was carried inside the coach, and baggage in a rack on top or in a "boot" on the back.

In movies and TV we always see the stagecoaches racing along as the horses run at a top speed gallop. But obviously no horses could sustain such a pace over

A stage coach and, right, two major coach routes.

the long and rugged miles between way stations. The stage drivers, however, liked to show off by galloping their teams out of a town, and whipping them up into a gallop as they entered the next one. But for most of the way in between the horses went along at a steady walk.

How was the Pony Express used? The bull trains that made the trip from Missouri to California in about two months, were fast enough for hauling freight. The stagecoaches, which took a few weeks to make the same journey, were all right for passengers. But both were too slow for important mail.

So Russell, Majors & Waddell decided to set up a super-fast mail service across the continent, which they called the Pony Express. They hired the finest riders in the West and mounted them on the fastest horses money could buy. These men carried the mail at a dead run over the entire two-thousand-mile run from St. Joe to California. The total time for the trip was nine days.

A pony express rider leaves a relay station.

The Camel Corps was a short-lived idea of spanning the gap between the east and west coasts of America.

There was a relay station every fifteen miles along the way. At every station, the rider changed to a fresh pony. Each rider normally covered a forty-five mile route. Then, the next day, he made the return trip to his home base.

The mail was carried in saddle bags, and each rider's load was limited to twenty pounds. In order to get as much mail as possible within the twenty-pound limit, most letters were written on tissue paper, as are many airmail letters today.

Among the first of the Pony Express riders was a teen-age boy named Bill Cody. Years later, as a buffalo hunter, an Indian scout, and the owner of the first Wild West show, he became world famous as Buffalo Bill.

Since transportation was so important to the winning of the West, all kinds of ideas were tried. During the 1850s, somebody in Washington got the notion that

When were camels used in the West?

33

if camels were so dependable for freighting goods across the Sahara Desert in Africa, they could serve equally well on the great American desert.

Accordingly, the U.S. Army sent a mission to Tunisia to buy a herd of camels, and the Camel Corps was formed. The fact that the corps failed was not the fault of the camels. They did their work well on several trips between Texas and California. The chief trouble was that American drivers, accustomed as they were to horses, mules and oxen, were baffled when it came to handling camels.

The Camel Corps gradually faded away. Some of the animals were sold to farmers, who tried vainly to teach them how to pull wagons and plows. The rest were turned loose in the desert to fend for themselves. None of them survived.

What was the Singing Wire?

Samuel F. B. Morse, a portrait painter with a flair for science, invented the "electric telegraph" in 1837. Five years later, with financial help from the Federal Government, the first long-distance line was strung between Baltimore and Washington.

In 1860, Congress appropriated money to stretch a telegraph line all the way across the country to the Pacific. The contract was given to the Western Union Company.

It was a long and backbreaking job. Sometimes poles had to be carried several hundred miles across the treeless plains and deserts. But the job was done in the amazing time of two years, and at last the East and the West were connected by a system of instant communication. The telegraph, of course, immediately put the Pony Express out of business.

The Indians were in awe of the telegraph. They believed that it was some kind of white man's magic, and they called the line the "singing wire."

What was the Golden Spike?

Ever since the first steam locomotive was built, men had dreamed of rails that could link the East and West. But the difficulties seemed in-

The invention of the "electric telegraph" in 1837 was an amazing step forward. The interiors of the first telegraph offices were a far cry from the streamlined Western Union operations today.

The builders of the railroad had not only to fight the difficulties of the terrain, but very often the Indians as well.

surmountable. True, by the 1840s, a line had been laid through the Alleghenies from Baltimore to Cumberland, Maryland. But building a railroad up and over the Rockies still seemed impossible. And even more impossible was the problem of getting over the practically vertical cliffs of the high Sierras that formed the eastern border of California.

But by 1862, while the Civil War was still raging, President Abraham Lincoln signed the Pacific Railroad Act that provided for Federal funds to build the road. The job was divided between two major railway companies. The Union Pacific was to build westward from Omaha. The Central Pacific was to build eastward from Sacramento. The government loaned the companies sums up to $48,000 per mile for the construction work, as well as granting them large segments of public lands along the right-of-way.

The Central Pacific, at first, had the toughest assignment, that of building a roadway through the canyons of the Sierras. To do this, they imported thousands of Chinese coolies. In some places these men were lowered from the tops of cliffs in wicker baskets to drill holes in the rock for blasting. Needless to say, the death toll was terrifyingly high. But the lives of coolies meant nothing to the ruthless and determined men who wanted to push the railroad through as fast as they could.

The Union Pacific also imported laborers, most of them from Ireland. Their greatest danger was from bands of hostile Indians, who constantly attacked the working parties.

Buffalo Bill Cody got his name when he was employed by the Union Pacific to hunt buffaloes as food for the crews. He and the hunters who assisted

On May 10, 1869, at Promontory Point, Utah, the last spike, made out of solid gold, was driven into the last tie. This marked the completion of the first transcontinental railroad.

him killed as many as a hundred of these unfortunate animals in one day.

The two lines met at last, on May 10, 1869, at Promontory Point, Utah. The final spike was made of gold, and it was driven by Leland Stanford, president of the Central Pacific. Legend has it that on his first try, he swung and missed. But finally he drove the golden spike into the tie, and the transcontinental railroad was complete.

Now, at last, the long trip from Omaha to San Francisco could be made in four days at an average speed of thirty miles an hour. This was a long step forward from the days of the cumbersome bull trains of only a few short years before.

Buffalo hunters supplied the food for the railroad crews.

The Cattle Country

Because of the superabundance of novels, short stories, movies, and TV shows that have been written about him, the cowboy of the Old West has become a legendary American hero. The image that is projected of him today is, of course, half fiction. But it is based on fact. The cowboy, as he existed in real life, was a very rugged and an extremely hard-working individual.

From where did the first cattle come?

Almost the entire West, from Nebraska to California, is natural cattle country. The thick grasslands of the Central Plains are the finest grazing lands in the world. Even in such semi-desert country as some parts of West Texas, Utah and New Mexico, cattle thrive on the scattered clumps of bunchgrass. As you drive across the Golden Gate Bridge from San Francisco, you can see cattle grazing on the slopes within plain view of one of America's greatest cities.

Cattle were first brought to California by the Spaniards, who herded them east into Texas and south into Mexico. They were slaughtered mainly for their hides which were shipped around Cape Horn to eastern ports.

Texans made a few scattered drives to the markets of St. Louis and New Orleans. But with the coming of the railroads into the West after the Civil War, cattle became big business. Ranchers in Texas pooled their herds into great drives that numbered thousands of head, and drove them north over such routes as the Chisholm Trail to railheads at Abiline, Sedalia or Dodge City. From there they were loaded on trains in special cattle-cars and shipped to the beef-hungry East.

In the early days, cattle ran wild on the unfenced range. In order to identify his own stock, each rancher had an individual brand-mark that he burned into the skin of his own animals. Then, usually twice a year, all the ranchers got together and rounded up their cattle. At the round-up they separated the cows according to their brands.

Why were cattle branded?

Strictly speaking, "cows" are the females of the bovine kingdom, as opposed to bulls, oxen or steers. But in the Old West, all cattle were referred to as cows, or cow-brutes.

Needless to say, many unscrupulous ranchers got rich by putting their brands on unbranded cows, or changing the brands that were already there. This business of cattle stealing was considered a serious offense in the Old West where cattle were the only wealth, and more often than not when the rustlers were caught, they were hanged from the nearest tree.

The cowboy did not refer to himself as a "cowboy." Instead, he called himself a cowpoke, a puncher, or, more commonly, a rider. The latter term resulted from the fact that he spent all of his working day, which usually extended from twelve to fifteen hours, in the saddle. He dressed for comfort and utility, not for style.

How did the cowboy dress?

He wore tight-fitting, blue canvas

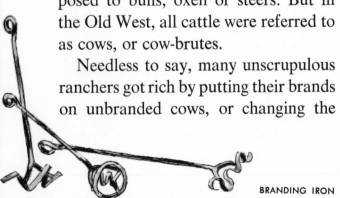

BRANDING IRON

hot summer sun, and from rain and snow in bad weather. Around his neck he wore a large bandana handkerchief that he could pull up over his nose for protection against the dust of the drives.

What was a cow pony?

There were no horses anywhere in North America until the Spanish conquerors came to Mexico and California. Inevitably, some of their war horses escaped and roamed free in herds over the plains. The Indians captured some of them and tamed them for riding, as did the early white men in the west. These semi-wild horses were small, but they were tough and agile. The cowboys called them mustangs, or broncos.

The cattlemen crossbred these mustangs with thoroughbred or standardbred horses from the East, and the result was the ideal horse for working cows. They were intelligent, fast on their feet, and quick to learn. They are known as quarter horses because no horse in the world could outrace them over a quarter-mile course.

The western saddle that the cowboy used was a heavy, cumbersome affair, but it was exactly what he needed for his work. The heavy horn in front was an anchor for his rope when he was snubbing a reluctant cow, or dragging a wagon out of the mud. The leather thongs that hung down all over the saddle held his lasso, bed-roll, slicker, and whatever other equipment he required.

pants, called "levis" because they had been designed and made by a man named Levi Strauss. When he was in rough brush country, he wore broad leather leggings over his levis, called chaps. His shirt was cotton, because there was no other kind on the frontier. He wore a vest instead of a coat because a sleeveless vest left his arms free.

On his feet he wore high-heeled boots. The high heels gave his feet more security in the stirrups, but they were uncomfortable for walking. On the heels of the boots he strapped big round Mexican spurs. His hat had a wide brim to protect his face and neck from the

Cowboys dressed for comfort, not for style.

Theodore Roosevelt loved to live a cowboy's life.

BRANDING THE CATTLE

Breaking-in a horse was no easy task. But once accomplished, man and animal formed an ideal team.

Roping of the calves on roundup day required the skill and strength of horse and rider.

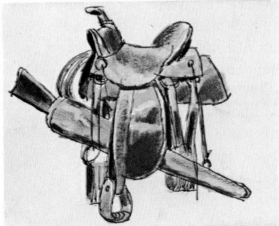

Although the Western saddle was heavy, it was exactly what the cowboy needed for his work.

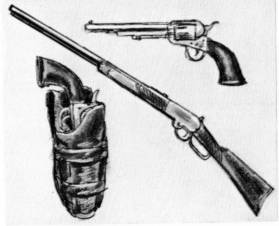

The Colt and the Winchester became the characteristic weapons of the cowboy of the cattle country.

Almost all cowboys carried guns; a rifle

Why did cowboys carry guns?

in a scabbard was attached to his saddle, and a revolver in a holster was strapped around his waist. These weapons protected him against rattlesnakes, wildcats or wolves that might molest him or his cattle, and against roving Indian war parties.

The most popular rifle in the West was the lever-action Winchester. The favorite pistol was the single-action Colt, later to be known as the Peacemaker. Both weapons were usually chambered for the .44 caliber cartridge. Thus the cowboy did not have to carry two kinds of ammunition. These two weapons played an important part in the eventual winning of the West.

There were many cowboys who later

Who was the cowboy-President?

became famous men. Tom Mix was a real-life cowboy before he became a movie cowboy. So was Gary Cooper. But the most famous of all the western cowboys was a young fellow named Teddy Roosevelt. He had gone to the Dakotas for his health and fallen in love with the rugged frontier life. He bought a ranch and worked on it for many years, sharing all the hardships of the other punchers who helped him run his cattle.

The hard work and the clean mountain air restored his health, and he later went back East to enter politics. In 1901, he became the 24th President of the United States.

Outlaws and Peace Officers

Ranking even higher than the cowboy

What were the cattle country crimes?

as an American folk-hero, are the western "bad men" and their enemies, the peace officers, who maintained order.

The early West was filled with rough, tough, disorderly men. Many of them were veterans of both armies in the Civil War, and had become hardened to killing. They preferred the easy life of robbing and cattle rustling to the hard work of the cattleman.

We have seen that stealing cattle was

JESSE JAMES

BILLY THE KID

WYATT EARP

BAT MASTERSON

CALAMITY JANE

WILD BILL HICKOK

usually punished at the end of a rope. But horse stealing was an even worse offense. Without his horse, a man would soon die on the endless, trackless plains. To steal a man's horse was almost the same as sentencing him to death. While mercy was occasionally shown to the rustler, the horse thief was hanged as soon as he was caught.

And yet many many of these bad men, because of their daring deeds, have become heros of song and legend.

Jesse James and his brothers specialized in robbing banks in small western towns. They would ride into a town on a day when it was sure to be nearly empty. Then they would shoot it up and in the general excitement break into the local bank and clean it out.

The Reno brothers were the first organized gang of train robbers. They would first spot a train that was due to be carrying a gold shipment. Then, in a remote place, they would pile ties, rocks and logs across the tracks. When the engineer brought the train to a stop, the robbers usually would kill the crew and terrorize the passengers, then escape with the cash box.

Other "family" gangs were the Daltons, the Doolins, the Youngers, the Farringtons, the McLauries, and the Clantons.

William Bonney (Billy the Kid) was a half-witted hoodlum who gained his reputation as a gunman by ambushing people or shooting them in the back. He was killed in a face-to-face fight with Sheriff Pat Garrett. John Wesley Hardin was a gunman, who later reformed and became a lawyer. Doc Holliday was a dentist who went West for his health and shortly made a name for himself as a notorious gambler and gunslinger. Al Jennings was a noted train robber, who saw the evil of his ways and in later years actually ran for governor of Oklahoma. But he was defeated.

Many of the gangs included women, who were just as ready to shoot down a victim as were the men. Among the most famous of these were Calamity Jane, Belle Starr, Poker Alice, and Cattle Annie.

The most effective law enforcement organization in the Old West was the Pinkerton Detective Agency. This agency had been formed during the Civil War to act as the secret service branch of the Union Army. But the Pinkertons, because they operated as a group, have been overshadowed by the individual lawmen.

Who kept the peace in the West?

Every western cow-town and mining town had its sheriff or marshal. The most famous of these were Wyatt Earp,

Bat Masterson, Wild Bill Hickok, Pat Garrett, Jim Cook, and Luke Short.

Most of the lawmen shot to kill only when it was absolutely necessary. Wyatt Earp carried a Colt revolver, known as a Buntline Special, which had a barrel twelve inches long. His favorite method of subduing a troublemaker was to whip this pistol out of its holster and hit the man over the head.

Perhaps the most famous of the battles between bad men and law men took place at the O.K. Corral, in Tombstone, Arizona, in October of 1881. Wyatt Earp, then the marshal of Tombstone, was challenged to a "shootout" by Ike and Billy Clanton, Frank and Tom McLaury, and Billy Claiborne. The outlaws said they would be waiting in the corral at the end of the town's main street. To help him, Wyatt took his two brothers, Virgil and Morgan, and the notorious Doc Holliday.

The fight lasted only a few minutes. When it was over Frank and Tom McLaurey and Billy Clanton were

dead. Billy Claiborne was badly wounded. Virgil Earp was nipped by a bullet in the leg and Morgan Earp in the shoulder.

The only outlaw who went unharmed was Ike Clanton, the leader of the gang. When the showdown came, he had been too frightened to draw his gun.

The Sod Busters

During the 1860s, Congress passed a law called the **What was the Homestead Act?** Homestead Act. This law provided that any man could stake out a claim to 160 acres of government-owned land in the West. After living on it for five years, he would become the legal owner.

During the depression years of the '70s and '80s, thousands of farmers from the crowded East came West to build a new future on the unplowed plains. They fenced in their 160 acres with barbed wire, built a house of blocks of sod, and began to plow up the grasslands to plant their fields of corn and wheat.

Since the cattlemen had always freely

Cattlemen try to bust through the fence of homesteaders to force them to relinquish their claims to the land.

used the government land as pasturage for their stock, a conflict was created that later led, in some instances, to open warfare. In addition to plowing up the land, many of the homesteaders brought in flocks of sheep that ate the grass down to its very roots and ruined it for cattle.

The big cattle barons were rich, and the homesteaders were extremely poor. During the first few years, the sodbusters had a hard time of it. It was difficult to find water on the plains. There were few streams, and sometimes the farmers had to dig down two or three hundred feet before they found underground water. They built windmills to draw it up.

Wood for fuel was another problem. There were no trees on the prairies except along the rivers, and so the settlers burned buffalo chips, and later cattle chips, the sun-dried droppings of these animals. It was a hard and lonely life.

During the first years, many of the sodbusters gave up their claims because of the constant pressure of the cowmen who often deliberately drove their herds through the homesteader's fields, and because of the hardships of operating a small farm in the wild lands of the West.

But enough of the farmers persisted until at last a compromise was reached. Today the Great Plains blossom with vast fields of grain and lush pasture land for sheep and cattle.

The Last of the Indian Wars

SITTING BULL

In retrospect most of us will praise the historical developments resulting from the fact that the white men dispossessed the Indians of their plains and mountain ranges and transformed the United States into a potentially very powerful nation. But while the white men were acquiring these western lands for the new nation,

What led to the Indian uprising?

the Indians were often subject to cruel and unjust treatment.

The Plains Indians indeed deserved the name "Noble Redmen." When they gave their word, they kept it. It was the white man who constantly broke his.

In return for being allowed to move onto the Indians' hunting grounds, the government promised that the settlers would advance just so far and no farther. Then the lush lands to the West beckoned, and the settlers kept moving in defiance of their agreements. The U.S. Army backed them up. Reluc-

46

tantly at first, and then with grim determination, the Indians fought for their hunting grounds.

The reason for the Indian Wars is simple. To the Plains Indians — the Sioux, Arapahoe, Commanche, Pawnee, Crow, Shoshone and other related tribes — the vast herds of buffalo that roamed over the prairie were their whole life. They ate its flesh. They made their tents and clothing from its hide. They used its bones for needles and knives, and its sinews for thread.

Before the flood of pioneers to the West after the Civil War, buffalo numbered in the tens of millions. They covered the plains in places like a great brown moving carpet. But when the white man came, he slaughtered these magnificent beasts ruthlessly. Usually he took only the hides, leaving the carcasses to rot. When the railroad construction crews started coming through, hunters like Buffalo Bill killed the animals by the thousands to provide food for the workers.

What was the Indian's last trail?

So the Indians had no choice but to fight to protect the buffalo that were their sole means of existence. And the U.S. Army fought back. In a few battles where they outnumbered the American soldiers, the Indian warriors won. At Little Big Horn, famous as Custer's Last Stand, Sitting Bull, the Sioux chief, and his men slaughtered all that remained of the famed Seventh Cavalry.

But the odds were sadly against the Indians. They could not hope to con-

The Indian chief, Wovoka, his head covered in shame, tells his people to travel the white man's road.

quer the whole American Army. Their last mass resistance took place at the Battle of Wounded Knee Creek in the Badlands of South Dakota. More than 200 Indians and some 60 U.S. soldiers were killed.

After Wounded Knee, the Indian wars finally came to the end of their blood-stained trail. Exhausted from years of resisting, the last of the Indian leaders, Wovoka, covered his head with a blanket to conceal his shame, and said to his people: "My children, today I call upon you to travel a new trail — the only trail still open — the white man's road."

The Indians went quietly back to the reservations that their conquerors had provided for them. Now the Indian wars were over. The white man owned and ruled the West.

April 22, 1889: The run into the Cherokee strip has begun.

The Cherokee Strip

The last great parcel of unsettled land in the West was a vast tract called the Cherokee Strip, which is now the state of Oklahoma. By the terms of an earlier treaty, it had been assigned as hunting grounds for the Cherokees, Choctaws, Chickasaws, Seminoles and Creeks, commonly called the Civilized Tribes. They had been promised that they would not be disturbed by white settlers.

Why was this the last frontier?

But by 1889, the pressure of settlers seeking new land was so great the government in Washington could not ignore it. President Benjamin Harrison proclaimed that the land would be opened for settlement. No one could enter the territory before 12 noon, April 22, 1889, the President proclaimed, but from that hour on it was every man for himself.

On the morning of the Run, as it was called, more than 10,000 people were lined up on the border of the Strip. Some rode fast horses; others had buggies or farm wagons. Promptly at high noon, an Army officer fired a starting gun, and the race started.

By the end of the week, the last of the Indians' land had been parceled out into farms, ranches and town sites. The state of Oklahoma had been born on the West's Last Frontier.